KETO ASIAN COOKBOOK:
WITH 10+ LOW CARB ASIAN RECIPES!

MW01602105

Table of Contents

Introduction

One of the most notable advantages of following a ketogenic diet is the increased production of ketones. These substances are present in greater levels in a person's blood when they are on a low-carb, high-fat diet. Ketones can also be used as an alternative energy source by cells that do not have access to glucose or fatty acids. These include heart and brain cells and cells that actively burn fat for fuel, such as skeletal muscle and the kidneys.

The fats that you consume in food are actually broken down into ketone bodies that can be used as fuel up to 80% of the time. This is why it takes more energy from carbohydrates to continue your day by day activities than fats and proteins. However, this doesn't mean that eating more protein will amount more energy for the body because proteins are also converted into glucose in the liver which is used as fuel instead of fat. So, to put it simply, a ketogenic diet helps you lose weight by taking your body's fuel (the glucose) and using fat instead which is a much better form of fuel as compared to glucose since it can be stored as fat and burn it when you don't eat carbs or are exercising.

The ketogenic diet is usually well-tolerated. Many studies have shown that there are very few side effects of following this way of eating. However, it can be strict depending on how much you change your eating habits. There may be some discomfort as you adapt to a new way of eating. However, this should pass after about three weeks. As long as you are following the plan correctly and not ignoring any of the foods which you shouldn't be consuming, then you will most likely remain healthy throughout your dieting period.

There are many different variations of the ketogenic diet and it can be used for more than just weight loss. It can help to achieve optimum health and well-being, reduce the risk of a range of chronic diseases, improve brain function and prevent age-related diseases including Alzheimer's disease, dementia and Parkinson's disease.

The ketogenic diet has been proven to be an effective treatment for epileptic conditions. This includes children who have suffered seizures due to epilepsy. The ketogenic diet works because it reduces the amount of glucose that is processed by your liver into insulin which is then released into your bloodstream.

Keto Asian Recipes

1. Pork with Ginger and Soy Sauce

Preparation Time: 10 minutes

Cooking Time: 15 minutes

Servings: 2

Ingredients:

- 9 ounces pork tenderloin, cut into chunks
- Black pepper, to taste
- 1 teaspoon cornstarch
- 2 tablespoons cold water
- 2 tablespoons dark soy sauce
- 2 tablespoons cooking oil
- 5½ ounces button mushrooms, sliced
- 1 medium red bell pepper, deseeded and sliced
- 2½ ounces snow peas, trimmed
- ¼ cup fresh ginger, peeled and julienned

- 1 clove garlic, thinly sliced
- 4 spring onions, sliced

Directions:

1. Season pork with black pepper.

2. In a small bowl, combine cornstarch with water and soy sauce. Set aside.

3. Heat 1 tablespoon oil in a wok, skillet, or frying pan.

4. Cook the pork until browned on the surface. Transfer pork to a plate.

5. Add remaining oil to the still-hot wok.

6. Stir-fry onion and pepper for 2 minutes.

7. Add the snow peas and stir-fry for 1 minute.

8. Add the ginger, garlic, and spring onion. Stir-fry briefly until fragrant.

9. Pour in soy mixture with the pork.

10. Cook until pork is done and sauce is thickened.

Nutrition:

Calories: 448

Carbs: 12.8 g

Fat: 24.7 g

Protein: 41.8 g

2. Pork in Black Bean Sauce

Preparation time: 15 minutes

Cooking Time: 20 minutes

Servings: 4

Ingredients:

- 1 pork tenderloin, about 1 ½ pounds, sliced thinly
- 4 tablespoons black bean sauce (easily obtained from most supermarkets)
- 1 tablespoon rice wine vinegar
- 1 teaspoon Chinese 5 spice powder
- 1 teaspoon cinnamon
- 3 tablespoons grapeseed oil, divided

- 1 teaspoon sesame oil
- 4 green onions, chopped
- 4 shallots, thinly sliced diagonally
- 1 cup mushrooms, sliced
- 1 red bell pepper, trimmed and chopped
- 2 cups of brown or white rice for serve (optional)

Directions:

1. Combine the pork, black bean sauce, rice wine vinegar, Chinese 5 spice powder, and cinnamon in a large bowl. Cover with either plastic wrap or a towel and marinate for at least 2 hours in the fridge.

2. While the meat is marinating, heat half of the grapeseed oil in a wok over medium heat. Sauté the shallots first until tender then add the green onions, mushrooms, and bell pepper. Add sesame oil and sauté for 4 minutes or until tender. Transfer to a plate.

3. After 2 hours, take the pork out of the fridge. Heat the remaining grapeseed oil in a wok over high heat. Add ¼ of the pork mixture and stir-fry for 3 minutes or until brown. Keep adding the pork in batches until ready.

4. Add the vegetable mixture and stir-fry for 2 minutes or until until warm.

5. Serve over rice, if desired.

Nutrition:

Calories: 488

Fat: 20.5 g

Carbohydrates: 10.4 g

Protein: 37 g

3. Shrimp in Lobster Sauce

Preparation Time: 10 minutes

Cooking Time: 15 minutes

Servings: 4

Ingredients:

- ¾ pound raw large shrimp, shelled and deveined
- Salt, to taste
- Sugar, to taste
- 2 tablespoons vegetable oil
- 1-inch piece ginger, peeled and chopped
- 2 cloves garlic, thinly sliced
- 1 cup chicken broth
- ½ tablespoon Chinese cooking wine
- ¾ cup frozen peas and carrots

- ¼ teaspoon white pepper
- ½ tablespoon light soy sauce
- 1 egg white, lightly beaten

For the Thickener:

- 1 tablespoon cornstarch
- 2 tablespoons water

Directions:

1. Season shrimp with salt and sugar. Set aside.

2. Stir ingredients for thickener in a small bowl or cup. Set aside.

3. Heat oil in a wok, skillet, or frying pan over medium heat.

4. Stir-fry ginger and garlic until fragrant (1–2 minutes).

5. Add shrimp and stir-fry until surface begins to turn opaque.

6. Pour in broth and cooking wine.

7. Bring to a boil.

8. Stir in frozen vegetables, white pepper, and soy sauce.

9. Adjust flavor, as needed, with salt and sugar.

10. Give the thickener a quick stir and gently pour into wok, stirring continuously.

11. Bring to a boil.

12. Drop egg into mixture and swirl three times with chopsticks or a spoon until whites form threads.

13. Immediately remove from heat.

14. Serve with rice.

Nutrition:

Calories: 276

Carbs: 7 g

Fat: 12 g

Protein: 32 g

4. Mu Shu Pork

Preparation Time: 10 minutes plus 15–20 minutes soaking and marinating time

Cooking Time: 5 minutes

Servings: 2

Ingredients:

- A pinch dried wood ear mushrooms
- ¼ cup dried lily flowers
- 4½ ounces pork tenderloin, sliced thinly across the grain

- 3 tablespoons peanut oil
- 2 eggs, beaten
- ¼ white onion, sliced
- ½ teaspoon minced ginger
- ½ seedless cucumber, sliced thinly and diagonally

For the Marinade:

- 2 teaspoons Chinese cooking wine
- ¼ teaspoon sea salt
- A dash white pepper powder
- ½ teaspoon cornstarch

For the Sauce:

- ¼ cup chicken stock
- 1 tablespoon light soy sauce
- ½ teaspoon Chinese black vinegar
- ½ teaspoon sesame oil
- Sea salt, to taste
- 1 teaspoon cornstarch

Directions:

1. Rehydrate the dried ingredients. Place mushroom and lily flowers in separate bowls. Cover each with hot water. Let soak for 30 minutes, keeping the water warm. Drain and trim off tough ends. Set aside.

2. In a medium bowl, mix together marinade ingredients except for the cornstarch. Add the pork and toss well. Add cornstarch and rub on surface until a thin film evenly covers the pork slices. Let marinate for 15 minutes.

3. In a small bowl, mix together sauce ingredients. Set aside.

4. Swirl 2 tablespoons oil in a wok, skillet, or frying pan and heat to almost smoking.

5. Lay pork pieces in wok and let cook for a few seconds.

6. When the underside is browned, flip over and let other side cook until white. Transfer to a plate, letting oil drip back, leaving about 1 tablespoon of oil in the wok.

7. Add more oil, if needed, and add beaten eggs. Let set and then stir until cooked through. Remove eggs and add to pork.

8. Add onion and ginger and stir-fry just until fragrant.

9. Add rehydrated mushrooms and lily flowers. Stir to coat with oil.

10. Add sauce and cook until thickened.

11. Return pork and egg to wok.

12. Stir in cucumber.

13. Season with salt, as needed.

14. Serve over rice.

Nutrition:

Calories: 376

Carbs: 9.6 g

Fat: 27.1 g

Protein: 23.8 g

Sodium 691 mg

5. Chicken with Sesame and Leek

Preparation Time: 5 minutes

Cooking Time: 15 minutes

Servings: 4

Ingredients:

- 1 tablespoon vegetable oil
- 2 teaspoons sesame oil
- 1½ pounds boneless, skinless chicken breast, cut into bite-size pieces
- 2 cloves garlic, minced
- 1 leek, cut into thin half-moons, rinsed and drained on paper towels
- 2 tablespoons soy sauce
- 1 tablespoon Mirin or Chinese cooking wine
- 1 teaspoon sugar

- 2 tablespoons toasted sesame seeds
- Salt and pepper, to taste
- Green onions, chopped, for garnish

Directions:

1. Heat the vegetable and sesame oils in a wok, skillet, or frying pan over high heat.

2. Swirl the oil to coat the wok and add the chicken (you may have to do this in batches).

3. Stir-fry the chicken until browned on the outside.

4. Stir in the garlic and leek and cook until the leek is tender (about 3 minutes).

5. Cover, reduce heat, and let simmer until chicken is cooked through.

6. Stir in soy sauce, Mirin, sugar, and sesame seeds. Cook until everything is heated through.

7. Adjust flavor with salt and pepper, as needed.

8. Sprinkle with chopped green onion and serve over rice or noodles.

Nutrition:

Calories: 157

Carbs: 8.7 g

Fat: 10.0 g

Protein: 8.8 g

6. Korean Chili Crab (Kkotgge Jjim)

Preparation Time: 10–15 minutes

Cooking time: 15 minutes

Servings: 1–2

Ingredients:

- 7 ounces (about 3–4) blue or flower crabs, cleaned, scrubbed
- Green and red chili peppers (optional)
- Sauce:
- ½ teaspoon Doenjang
- 1½ tablespoons Gochujang
- 1¼ cups water
- 4 large dried anchovies

- 3 tablespoons soy sauce
- 1 tablespoon Gochugaru
- 1 tablespoon Mirin
- 1 tablespoon soy sauce
- ½ teaspoon grated ginger
- 1 clove garlic, finely minced
- Few pinches of pepper

Directions:

1. Brush the crabs and rinse well. Remove the legs and reserve the claws.
2. Open up the back tab towards the front and remove it from the crab.
3. You will notice yolk-like eggs inside. Take them out and place them on the removed top shell.
4. Discard the grey gills and clean and rinse the crabs.
5. Add the water, Doenjang and anchovies to a deep saucepan or cooking pot; boil over medium-high heat for 5 minutes.
6. Remove the anchovies and reserve the stock in a bowl.
7. Add the sauce ingredients to the bowl and combine well.
8. Add the crabs and shells with eggs to the pot. Add the sauce on top.
9. Bring the mixture to a boil, then reduce heat to low, cover, and simmer for 5–7 minutes.
10. Serve with rice.

Nutrition:

Calories 167

Fat: 4 g

Carbs: 9 g

Protein: 10 g

7. Glazed Soybean Salmon

Preparation Time: 10 minutes

Cooking time: 15 minutes

Servings: 4

Ingredients:

- 1½ tablespoons mayonnaise
- 1 tablespoon honey
- 1½ pounds salmon fillets
- 2 tablespoons Doenjang
- 2 teaspoons finely minced garlic
- 1 tablespoon Mirin or dry sherry
- 1–2 tablespoons fresh parsley, finely chopped
- Few dashes hot sauce (optional)

Directions:

1. To make the sauce, combine all the Ingredients except for the salmon in a mixing bowl.
2. Preheat the oven to 400°F (204°C). Grease a baking dish with some cooking spray.
3. Add the salmon, top with the sauce, and bake for 15–18 minutes.
4. Serve warm with rice.

Nutrition:

Calories 124

Fat: 4 g

Carbs: 8 g

Protein: 6 g

8. Creamy Fruit Salad

Preparation Time: 10 minutes

Cooking time: 10 minutes

Servings: 6

Ingredients:

- 1 persimmon, peeled, cored, stemmed and cubed
- 1 red apple, cored and cubed
- 1 mandarin orange, peeled and separated
- 1 cucumber, seeded and cubed
- ⅓ cup raisins
- ¼ cup roasted salted peanuts or other nuts of your choice

Dressing

- 1–1½ teaspoons honey (or to taste)
- 1 teaspoon lemon juice

- 5 tablespoons mayonnaise
- Fine sea salt (optional)

Directions:

1. Combine the dressing Ingredients in a mixing bowl.
2. Add the persimmon and other Ingredients to another bowl.
3. Top with the dressing, toss well and serve fresh.

Nutrition:

Calories 118

Fat: 9 g

Carbs: 10 g

Protein: 1 g

9. Marinated BBQ Chicken

Preparation time: 15 minutes

Cooking time: 10 minutes

Servings: 6

Ingredients:

- 3 tablespoon tomato sauce
- ¼ cup soy sauce
- 2 tablespoon mirin
- 1 tablespoon rice vinegar
- 1 tablespoon orange zest
- 1 teaspoon sesame seeds
- 1 white onion
- ½ cup parsley
- 3 tablespoon butter
- 1 teaspoon honey
- 1 teaspoon salt

- 1 teaspoon ground black pepper
- 15 oz. chicken thigh

Directions:

1. Peel the onion and grate it.
2. Melt butter in the saucepan and add mirin, rice vinegar, orange zest, honey, salt, and ground black pepper.
3. Stir the mixture and remove it from the heat.
4. Peel the onion.
5. Chop the onion and parsley.
6. Add the chopped components in the saucepan.
7. Add soy sauce and tomato sauce.
8. Whisk the mixture and chill it well.
9. After this, mix the chicken tights with the sauce mixture well. Marinate it.
10. Preheat the grill and put the marinated chicken tights.
11. Cook the chicken tights for 5 minutes from the each side.
12. Serve the marinated BBQ chicken immediately.
13. Enjoy!

Nutrition:

Calories 212

Fat: 13.8

Carbs: 8.45

Protein: 14

10. Chicken Bulgogi

Preparation time: 10 minutes

Cooking time: 25 minutes

Servings: 8

Ingredients:

- 2 onions
- ¼ cup soy sauce
- 1 tablespoon brown sugar
- 3 garlic cloves
- 2 tablespoon olive oil
- 1 teaspoon cayenne pepper
- 1 teaspoon salt
- 1 teaspoon white pepper
- 2-pound chicken, boneless

Directions:

1. Peel the onion and chop it.
2. Toss the chopped onion in the skillet.
3. Add brown sugar, olive oil, cayenne pepper, salt, and white pepper.
4. Mix the mixture up.
5. After this, peel the garlic cloves and slice them.
6. Add the sliced garlic cloves in the skillet too.
7. Then add the soy sauce and preheat the mixture on the medium heat for 5 minutes.
8. Meanwhile, chop the chicken roughly.
9. Add the chopped chicken in the marinated mixture and simmer the dish for 20 minutes. Stir it frequently.
10. When the chicken bulgogi is cooked – serve the dish hot.
11. Enjoy!

Nutrition:

Calories: 193

Fat: 8

Carbs: 5.26

Protein: 24

11.   Tasty Braised Tofu

Preparation time: 10 minutes

Cooking time: 15 minutes

Servings: 7

Ingredients:

- 9 oz. tofu
- 1 teaspoon olive oil
- 1 teaspoon sesame seeds oil
- 1 tablespoon minced garlic
- ½ onion
- 1 teaspoon chili flakes
- 3 tablespoon soy sauce
- ¼ cup water

Directions:

1. Chop the tofu into the medium cubes.
2. Mix the olive oil and sesame seeds oil in the pan and preheat it.
3. Then add the tofu cubes in the preheat oil and cook them until the cheese is golden brown from the both sides.
4. Meanwhile, peel the onion and grate it.
5. Mix the grated onion with the minced garlic and soy sauce.
6. Add chili flakes and water. Stir the mixture.
7. Remove the cooked tofu from the pan and transfer the sauce to the remaining oil.
8. Cook the sauce until it is starting to boil.
9. After this, add the tofu cubes.
10. Braise the mixture for 5 minutes more.
11. When the dish is cooked – chill it well.
12. Serve the dish immediately.
13. Enjoy!

Nutrition:

Calories: 133

Fat: 9.5

Carbs: 6.9

Protein: 7

12. Sweet Carrot Salad

Preparation time: 15 minutes

Cooking time: 5 minutes

Servings: 4

Ingredients:

- 1 teaspoon lime zest
- 1 tablespoon lemon juice
- 1 teaspoon onion powder
- 1 garlic clove
- 1 teaspoon brown sugar
- 1 cup water
- 10 oz. carrot
- 1 tablespoon rice vinegar
- 2 teaspoon soy sauce

- 1 tablespoon Korean chili flakes

Directions:

1. Pour water into the saucepan and boil it.
2. Meanwhile, peel the carrot and cut it into the matchsticks.
3. Then place the carrot in the boiled water and blanch it for 3 minutes.
4. Strain the carrot and transfer it to the big bowl.
5. Sprinkle the blanched carrot with the lime zest, lemon juice, onion powder, brown sugar, rice vinegar, soy sauce, and Korean chili flakes.
6. Peel the garlic clove and chop it.
7. Sprinkle the carrot mixture with the chopped garlic and stir it with the help of the fork.
8. Then leave the salad for at least 10 minutes to marinate.
9. Serve the side dish and enjoy!

Nutrition:

Calories: 48

Fat: 0.9

Carbs: 9.74

Protein: 1

13.   Roasted Branzino

Preparation time: 15 minutes

Cooking time: 20 minutes

Servings: 3

Ingredients:

- 1-pound branzino
- ½ tablespoon salt
- 1 teaspoon ground white pepper
- 2 tablespoon scallion
- 1 teaspoon olive oil
- 2 tablespoon soy sauce
- 1 small onion
- 1 tablespoon fish sauce
- 1 teaspoon fresh ginger

- 1 tablespoon lemon juice
- 1 teaspoon minced garlic
- 1 teaspoon chili flakes

Directions:

1. Mix the salt, ground white pepper, and chili flakes.
2. Stir the mixture and rub the branzino with the spices.
3. Leave the fish for 10 minutes to marinate.
4. Meanwhile, peel the onion and chop it roughly.
5. Mix the fish sauce, fresh ginger, minced garlic, soy sauce, and olive oil together.
6. Stir the mixture and spread the fish with the mixture.
7. Preheat the oven to 365 F.
8. Put the branzino in the tray and transfer the tray to the oven.
9. Roast the fish for 12 minutes.
10. Chop the scallion and sprinkle the fish.
11. Then turn the fish to another side and cook it for 8 minutes not.
12. Serve the fish hot.
13. Enjoy!

Nutrition:

Calories: 292

Fat: 13.6

Carbs: 7.98

Protein: 33

14.   Soybean Soup

Preparation time: 15 minutes

Cooking time: 17 minutes

Servings: 10

Ingredients:

- 4 tablespoon soybean paste
- 1 teaspoon salt
- 1 red onion
- 8 oz. shiitake mushrooms
- 1 tablespoon chili paste
- 9 oz. tofu
- 9 cup fish stock
- ½ teaspoon minced garlic
- 10 oz. zucchini

- 1 teaspoon chili flakes

Directions:

1. Pour the fish stock into the saucepan.
2. Add salt, soy bean paste, and chili paste. Stir the mixture well.
3. Boil the liquid for 7 minutes.
4. Then strain the liquid and return it back into the saucepan.
5. Cut the zucchini into the strips and put them in the boiling liquid.
6. Peel the onion and dice it.
7. Add the diced onion to the soup and close the lid.
8. Cook the soup for 4 minutes.
9. After this, add minced garlic and chili flakes.
10. Cook the soup for 3 minutes.
11. Chop the tofu into the cubes and add it to the soup.
12. Cook the dish for 2 minutes more.
13. Then remove the soup from the heat and let it rest for 5 minutes.
14. Ladle the soup into the bowls.
15. Serve the soup immediately.
16. Enjoy!

Nutrition:

Calories: 129

Fat: 7.2

Carbs: 8.43

Protein: 11

15. Spinach Side Dish

Preparation time: 7 minutes

Cooking time: 5 minutes

Servings: 3

Ingredients:

- 3 cups spinach
- 3 cups water
- 1 teaspoon minced garlic
- 1 tablespoon sesame seeds
- 1 tablespoon olive oil
- 1 teaspoon Korean red pepper
- ½ white onion

Directions:

1. Wash the spinach carefully and put it in the saucepan.
2. Mix the water and salt together and stir it gently to make the salt dissolve.

3. Pour the salty water in the spinach and close the lid.

4. Blanche the spinach for 5 minutes or until it is half-soft.

5. After this, transfer the spinach to the colander and chill it well.

6. Then chop the blanched spinach roughly and transfer it to the big bowl.

7. Mix the minced garlic, sesame seeds, olive oil, and Korean red pepper together.

8. Dice the onion and add it to the minced garlic mixture.

9. Poach the mixture well.

10. Sprinkle the chopped spinach with the olive oil mixture.

11. Mix the spinach side dish well and serve it immediately.

12. Enjoy!

Nutrition:

Calories: 78

Fat: 6.3

Carbs: 4.84

Protein: 2

Conclusion

Thank you for making it to the end. So you're ready to try the Ketogenic Diet for weight loss, brain health, or maybe just a boost of energy! That's great; you're not alone. However, before diving into this new and exciting lifestyle change, there are a few things worth knowing before going too deep with the keto diet. This cookbook aims to cover some practical advice for those who are new to the Ketogenic Diet and have questions about what exactly it entails. It also provides tips on how to get started in making this lifestyle change - from choosing your meal plan (yes, truly planning your meals can be that easy) and staying on track until long term habits are set in motion.

The ketogenic diet, also known as the keto diet for short or the low carb diet, is a mainstream dietary therapy that has been used since the late 1920s to treat epilepsy in children. The diet is highly restrictive and involves high consumption of individual foods along with a moderate amount of protein. The only signifcant negative effect is that due to carbohydrate restriction, severe constipation may occur. For children it reduces seizure frequency by approximately 50% [1]but this effect can generally be circumvented by making your own keto friendly food such as low carb vegetables, meats, and starches that are consumed outside of the immediate post-meal period.

As we end this book, here are some tips:

- Get enough water. Unlike most diets, you can drink as much water as you want on the keto diet.

- Drink coffee or tea if you need a little caffeine fix, but try to stick to no more than three cups per day for maximum benefits to your weight loss efforts. You can also use artificial sweeteners (Stevia) in your drinks if you prefer them over sugar or honey for taste.

- Eat keto foods as often and as frequently as possible. If you are following a meal plan, stick to that plan but make changes, if needed, to accommodate your personal needs.

- Try eating eggs for breakfast. Adding one large hard boiled egg to your morning meal can provide you with the necessary protein that may help you feel fuller longer, resulting in improved weight loss success. If using hard-boiled eggs instead of raw eggs, be sure to wash them thoroughly to avoid food-borne illnesses.

- Instead of drinking sweetened or sugary beverages or adding sugar-sweetened foods, drink water and unsweetened tea or coffee with no sweeteners added. Artificial sweeteners do not offer any health benefits.

- If you are following a high-protein diet, make sure to eat one or two servings of fatty foods such as cheese or heavy cream per day. When you eat fatty foods, your body will burn the fat instead of carbohydrates for energy.

- Get enough sleep. It does not matter if you have a busy job and need to get eight hours or less of sleep each night, your body still needs the rest it needs to function properly and help with weight loss efforts. Even if you do not think that you need more than six hours of sleep each night that it is recommended to get a full eight hours of sleep each night while on the keto diet.

I hope you liked this book!

Made in the USA
Coppell, TX
15 February 2025

45975134R00024